W9-AWV-319

MAKING GRAPHS

Please visit our web site at: www.garethstevens.com
For a free color catalog describing Gareth Stevens Publishing's list
of high-quality books and multimedia programs, call 1-800-542-2595 (USA)
or 1-800-387-3178 (Canada). Gareth Stevens Publishing's fax: (414) 332-3567.

Library of Congress Cataloging-in-Publication Data

Nechaev, Michelle Wagner.
    Making graphs / written by Michelle Wagner Nechaev; photographed by Michael Jarrett. — North American ed.
      p. cm. — (I can do math)
    Summary: Uses foods, games, and stuffed animals to demonstrate graphing.
    ISBN 0-8368-4111-5 (lib. bdg.)
    1. Graphic methods—Juvenille literature. (1. Graphic methods.) I. Jarrett, Michael, 1956- ill. II. Title. III. Series.
QA90.N35   2004
001.4'226—dc22
                                            2003058387

This North American edition first published in 2004 by
Gareth Stevens Publishing
A World Almanac Education Group Company
330 West Olive Street, Suite 100
Milwaukee, WI 53212 USA

Original copyright © 1998 by Creative Teaching Press, Inc.
First published in the United States in 1998 as *Our Favorites* in the
Learn to Read -- Read to Learn Math Series by Creative Teaching
Press, Inc., P.O. Box 2723, Huntington Beach, CA 92647-0723.

Gareth Stevens series editor: Dorothy L. Gibbs
Gareth Stevens series designer: Kami M. Koenig

Printed in the United States of America

2 3 4 5 6 7 8 9 09 08 07 06 05

MAKING GRAPHS

Written by Michelle Wagner Nechaev
Photographed by Michael Jarrett

I CAN + DO MATH

Gareth Stevens Publishing
A WORLD ALMANAC EDUCATION GROUP COMPANY

cheese

bananas

apples

brownies

cupcakes

cookies

4

These are our favorite foods.
We can make graphs of our favorite foods.

We can use the colors
of the foods to make a graph.

6

We can use the first letters
of the foods to make a graph.

Can you think of other ways
to make graphs
of our favorite foods?

9

baseball

jacks

soccer

cards

basketball

video games

These are our favorite games.
We can make graphs of our favorite games.

We can make a graph of where
we play our favorite games.

We can make a graph of games
that use a ball and don't use a ball.

13

Can you think of other ways
to make graphs
of our favorite games?

15

horse

rooster

whale

fish

zebra

cow

monkey

dolphin

tiger

pig

shark

parrot

giraffe

16

These are our favorite animals.
We can make graphs of our favorite animals.

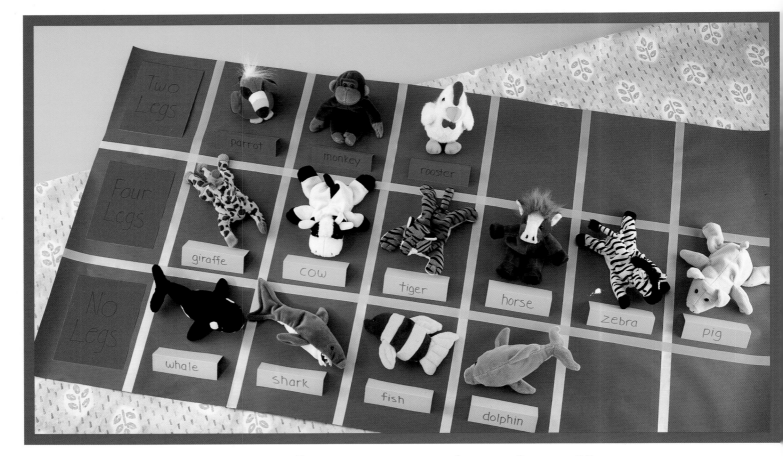

We can make a graph using the numbers of legs the animals have.

In the Sea	shark	dolphin	fish	whale
In the Wild	tiger	giraffe	zebra	monkey	parrot
On the Farm	pig	horse	rooster	cow	

We can make a graph of
where the animals live.

Can you think of other ways
to make graphs
of our favorite animals?

MATH QUIZ (answers on page 24)

1. If you use the tastes of the foods below to make a graph,

brownie

cookie

apple

cheese

cupcake

banana

cracker

A. which foods belong in the sweet group?

B. which foods belong in the salty group?

22

2. If you use the numbers of letters in the names

A. how many letter groups would you have to make?

B. which letter group would have the most animals in it?

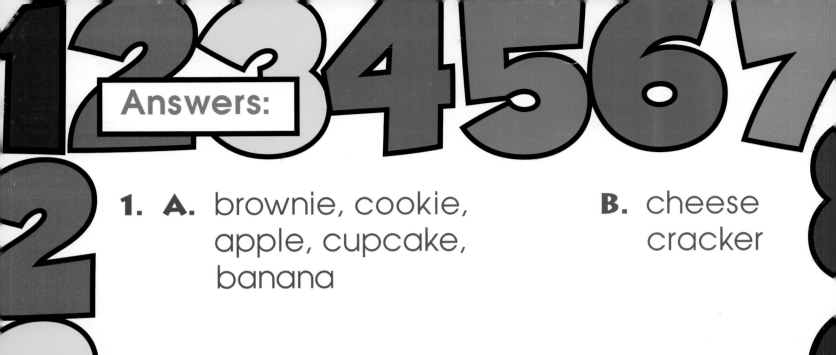

Answers:

1. A. brownie, cookie, apple, cupcake, banana

B. cheese cracker

2. A. 5 letter groups: Three Letters · Four Letters
Five Letters · Six Letters
Seven Letters

B. Five Letters